Contents

2 Place value
4 Ordering numbers
6 More ordering numbers
8 Writing numbers
10 Multiplication
12 Division
14 Checking your maths
16 Fractions
18 Measuring
20 Understanding time
22 Two- and three-dimensional shapes
24 Money
26 Quick test
28 Explorer's logbook
30 Answers
32 Certificate

Introduction

If you are wild about learning and wild about animals – this book is for you!

It will take you on a wild adventure, where you will practise key maths skills and explore the amazing world of animals along the way.

Each maths topic is introduced in a clear and simple way with lots of interesting activities to complete so that you can practise what you have learned.

Alongside every maths topic you will uncover fascinating facts about grassland animals.

When you have completed each topic, record the animals that you have seen and the skills that you have learned in the explorer's logbook on pages 28–29.

Good luck, explorer!

Alan Dobbs

Place value

All numbers are made from the digits **1**, **2**, **3**, **4**, **5**, **6**, **7**, **8**, **9** and **0** (zero).

If it is a **single-digit number**, then it has to be **0**, **1**, **2**, **3**, **4**, **5**, **6**, **7**, **8** or **9**.

In a **two-digit** number, like 23, the 2 has a **value** of 20 and the 3 is worth three ones. The 2 has a higher value than the 3, because of its **place** in the number. A zero is used as a place holder. The number 10 has a zero to show 1 lot of 10 and 0 ones.

By looking at the place of each number you can find its value.

An abacus can show numbers with different values. It uses beads to show each digit.

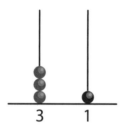

This abacus shows 3 lots of 10 and 1 lot of 1. The number is 31.

Task 1 Write each of these numbers, using the abacus beads to help you.

a  b 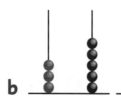 c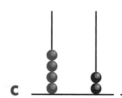

Task 2　Look at the single-digit numbers on the lions below.

a Use 2 of the single-digit numbers to make a two-digit number. _____

b Use 2 of the numbers to make the highest value two-digit number that you can. _____

c Now make the lowest value number, using 2 different numbers. _____

WILD FACT

Lions are the only wild cats that live together. A group of lions is called a pride.

Task 3　Write down the value of the underlined digit. The first two have been done for you.

2<u>1</u> 1

<u>4</u>6 40

a 3<u>6</u> _____

b <u>2</u>4 _____

c 5<u>7</u> _____

d <u>7</u>3 _____

e <u>4</u>5 _____

f <u>9</u>9 _____

WILD FACT

The female lions, or lionesses, do most of the hunting, but the male in the pride often arrives to steal the tasty parts!

Now pad over to pages 28–29 and record what you have learned in your explorer's logbook!

Ordering numbers

Understanding the **place** that a number has and which numbers would be **one more** and **one less** helps us to remember the **order** of numbers.

If the number is 12, then 1 more would be 13 and 1 less would be 11.

On a number line, it would look like this:

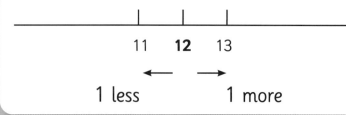

| | 11 | **12** | 13 |

1 less ← → 1 more

Task 1 Count the ostriches and write one more and one less of each set.

a 1 less _____   1 more _____

b 1 less _____   1 more _____

c 1 less _____   1 more _____

4

Task 2   Use the number line to answer these questions.

| | | | | | | | | | | | | | | | | | |
|13|14|15|16|17|18|19|20|21|22|23|24|25|26|27|28|29|30|

a Write the number that is one less than 16.   _____

b Which number is one more than 29?   _____

c Write the number that is one less than 24.   _____

d Which number is one more than 13?   _____

WILD FACT

The ostrich is the largest bird in the world. It has very strong legs and can run at 70 kilometres an hour to escape predators!

Task 3   Complete the grid to show one more and one less for each number shown.

1 less		1 more
	56	
	34	
	21	
	2	
	13	
	73	
	55	

WILD FACT

Ostriches have the largest eyes of any bird. Each eye is actually bigger than its brain!

Now sprint over to pages 28–29 and fill in your explorer's logbook!

5

More ordering numbers

FACT FILE

Animal: Black rhinoceros
I live in: African grassland
I weigh: Up to 1,400 kg
I eat: Leaves and fruit from trees and bushes

Look at these numbers: **12   7   23**

If they were in **order**, the numbers would look like this: **7   12   23** (**7** is the **lowest** and **23** is the **highest**).

Numbers can be ordered in different ways. The numbers below go from **highest** to **lowest**. They are still in an order, but the order is different.

12   8   5   3   1

Task 1	Put these numbers in order from lowest to highest.

a 14 26   3 32   12 _____

b 45 13   7   2   29 _____

c 16   3 23 21   60 _____

d 54 43 10 51   13 _____

Task 2 Put these numbers in order, from highest to lowest.

a 2 10 6 8 3 _____

b 16 20 4 34 18 _____

c 5 27 16 39 51 _____

Task 3 One of these lines has numbers that are **lowest to highest**. Put a tick in the box for this line.

5 9 3 10 12 ☐

12 14 16 18 20 ☐

10 7 4 3 1 ☐

Task 4 This line is counting from lowest to highest. Add the missing numbers.

2 ☐ 4 ☐ 6 ☐

WILD FACT
Black rhinoceros really enjoy rolling in the mud, as it helps them to keep cool and protects them from the sun.

WILD FACT
Rhinoceros horn is extremely strong. It is made out of keratin, which is what your hair and nails are made from.

Now charge over to pages 28–29 and fill in your explorer's logbook!

Writing numbers

FACT FILE
Animal: Dik-dik
I live in: African savannah and grassland
I weigh: Up to 6 kg
I eat: Plants, leaves and fruit

When you write a number as a **numeral**, it looks like a number. 1, 2 and 3 are numerals.

Numbers can also be written as **words**. For example, **one**, **two** and **three** are numbers written as words, and the number **10** written as a word is **ten**.

Task 1 Write these numbers as words.

a 8 _____

b 6 _____

c 12 _____

d 3 _____

Task 2 Write these words as numerals.

a five _____

b twenty _____

c eleven _____

d one _____

Task 3

Draw lines to match the words to their numerals.

sixteen	**9**
seven	**8**
nine	**16**
eight	**7**

WILD FACT

Dik-diks are so small that they sometimes need to stand on their back legs to reach the tasty leaves and fruit.

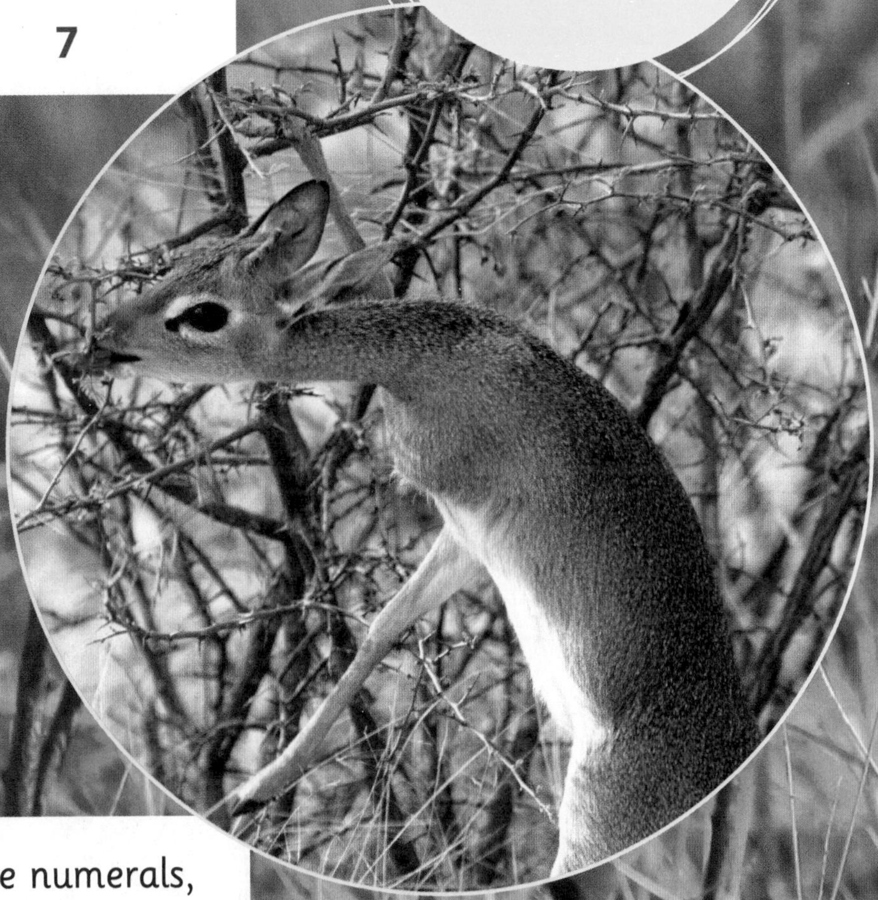

Task 4

Look at the numerals, then fill in the blanks to complete the words.

a 7 ___e___e___

b 14 f___u___t___e___

c 21 tw___n___y-___n___

d 43 ___o___ty-t___r___e

WILD FACT

Dik-diks don't need to drink water. They get all the moisture they need from the food they eat.

Now spring to pages 28–29 and fill in your explorer's logbook!

Multiplication

Numbers can be counted in different ways. **Multiplication** is the same as **repeated addition**.

2 × 3 is **3 lots of 2**, or the same as **2 + 2 + 2**. The answer for each calculation is **6**.

FACT FILE

Animal: Cape cobra
I live in: African deserts and savannah
I am: Up to 1.5 metres long
I eat: Small mammals, lizards, birds and eggs

Task 1 Write these multiplications as repeated additions. An example has been done for you.

2 × 4 (4 lots of 2) 2 + 2 + 2 + 2 (or 2 lots of 4) 4 + 4

a 5 × 3 _____

b 10 × 5 _____

c 2 × 6 _____

Task 2 Write these additions as multiplications. An example has been done for you.

$5 + 5 + 5 = \underline{5} \times \underline{3}$ or $\underline{3} \times \underline{5}$

a $10 + 10 + 10 + 10 + 10$ = _____

b $2 + 2 + 2 + 2 + 2 + 2 + 2$ = _____

c $5 + 5 + 5 + 5 + 5 + 5 + 5$ = _____

Task 3 Write the answers to these multiplications. An example has been done for you.

$5 \times 2 = 10$

a 2×5 = _____

b 10×6 = _____

c 2×8 = _____

WILD FACT

When frightened or attacking prey, a cape cobra will raise its body high into the air, hiss and unfold the flaps of skin on either side of its head, known as its hood.

WILD FACT

Cape cobras have a toxic bite that is powerful enough to kill a person within 30 minutes!

Task 4 Fill in the correct numbers to complete these multiplications.

a $3 \times \underline{} = 15$

b $\underline{} \times 2 = 12$

c $4 \times \underline{} = 16$

d $\underline{} \times 3 = 18$

Now slither over to pages 28–29 and fill in your explorer's logbook!

11

Division

FACT FILE

Animal: Zebra
I live in: African grassland
I weigh: Up to 450 kg
I eat: Grass

Dividing a number means **sharing** it into **equal amounts**. If you share 10 carrots between 2 zebras, each zebra would get 5 carrots. The calculation would look like this:

$$10 \div 2 = 5$$

You can find out other things by dividing a group by 2.

If you know that **6 ÷ 2 = 3** then you also know that there are **3 groups of 2 in 6!**

Task 1   Divide these carrots between 2 zebras. An example has been done for you.

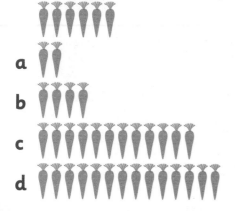

$$6 \div 2 = 3$$

a Write the calculation _____

b Write the calculation _____

c Write the calculation _____

d Write the calculation _____

Task 2

Look at the zebras and write down the division calculation and the answer.

 = _____

Task 3

How many sets of 2 are there in the groups of zebras?

a  = _____ sets of 2.

b 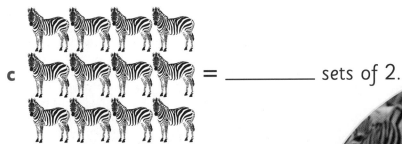 = _____ sets of 2.

c  = _____ sets of 2.

Now gallop to pages 28–29 and fill in your explorer's logbook!

Checking your maths

Addition (+) is the opposite of subtraction (−) and multiplication (×) is the opposite of division (÷).

You can check your addition calculations by using subtraction and multiplication calculations using division — and the other way round!

2 + 4 = 6 and **6 − 4 = 2**

Can you see that they are the same calculation, but opposite?

FACT FILE

Animal: Spotted hyena
I live in: African grassland and savannah
I weigh: Up to 85 kg
I eat: Wildebeest, antelopes, and I'll scavenge the leftovers of other animals

Task 1

Look at these additions and do the opposite subtraction. An example has been done for you.

$5 + 3 = 8$ $8 − 3 = 5$

a $2 + 1 = 3$ _____

b $6 + 1 = 7$ _____

c $4 + 6 = 10$ _____

WILD FACT

Hyenas live in large groups, known as 'clans'. A clan can have up to 130 animals in it. They communicate with each other by 'whooping', which sounds as if they are laughing!

Task 2

Now write these multiplications as divisions. An example has been done for you.

$2 \times 5 = 10$ $10 \div 5 = 2$

a $3 \times 2 = 6$ _____

b $4 \times 2 = 8$ _____

c $6 \times 2 = 12$ _____

Task 3

Write the opposite of these calculations. An example has been done for you.

$5 \times 2 = 10$ $10 \div 2 = 5$

a $2 + 10 = 12$ _____

b $10 \div 2 = 5$ _____

c $20 - 10 = 10$ _____

Now take your clan over to pages 28–29 and fill in your explorer's logbook!

Fractions

Fractions are equal parts of 1 whole.

This circle has been split into **2 equal parts**. Each part is 1 **half**, or $\frac{1}{2}$. One half is shaded.

This circle has been split into **4 equal parts**. Each part is a **quarter**, or $\frac{1}{4}$. One quarter is shaded.

Groups can also be split into halves ($\frac{1}{2}$). In this group of 4 bush babies, half ($\frac{1}{2}$) would be 2 bush babies.

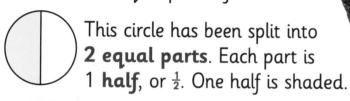

(Remember that the number in each half must be the same.)

Splitting into quarters is the same as halving and halving again. To split a group into quarters ($\frac{1}{4}$), there must be 4 equal parts. If you first split the group in half, and split each half in half again, you have 4 equal quarters.

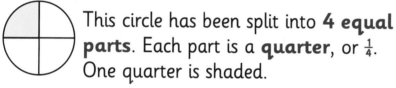

Task 1   Colour the correct fractions of each circle.

a $\frac{1}{2}$

b $\frac{1}{4}$

Task 2   Find half ($\frac{1}{2}$) of these groups of bush babies.

a   🐾🐾🐾🐾🐾🐾

$\frac{1}{2}$ = _____

b   🐾🐾🐾🐾🐾🐾🐾🐾

$\frac{1}{2}$ = _____

c   🐾🐾🐾🐾🐾🐾🐾🐾🐾🐾

$\frac{1}{2}$ = _____

WILD FACT

When hunting for food, bush babies fold back their big ears so that they don't get in the way as they leap from tree to tree.

WILD FACT

Bush babies may be small, but they can make a lot of noise! They make loud, high-pitched sounds, which sound very like a human baby.

Task 3   Find a quarter ($\frac{1}{4}$) of these groups of bush babies.

a   🐾🐾🐾🐾

$\frac{1}{4}$ = _____

b   🐾🐾🐾🐾🐾🐾🐾🐾

$\frac{1}{4}$ = _____

c   🐾🐾🐾🐾🐾🐾🐾🐾🐾🐾🐾🐾

$\frac{1}{4}$ = _____

Now climb over to pages 28–29 and fill in your explorer's logbook!

Measuring

We measure lots of things in lots of ways. **Length** (how long something is) and **height** (how tall something is) are measured in centimetres (cm) and metres (m). **Weight** (how heavy something is) is measured using grams (g) and kilograms (kg). **Capacity** (how much something holds) is measured using millilitres (ml) and litres (l).

Task 1

Look at this giraffe. It measures 4 metres (4 m). It is 4 m tall, or 4 m in height.

A   4 m

FACT FILE

Animal: Giraffe
I live in: Grasslands and
            woodlands of Africa
I am: Up to 8 metres tall!
I eat: Leaves and plants

Now look at this giraffe.
It measures 3 metres (3 m).
It is 3 m tall, or 3 m in height.

B   3 m

Which giraffe is taller, **A** or **B**? _____

Task 2

Giraffes eat lots of leaves. Each branch below has 1 kg of leaves on it.

Giraffe **A** eats this amount.

Giraffe **B** eats this amount.

a How many kg of leaves does each giraffe eat?

Giraffe **A** _____

Giraffe **B** _____

b Which giraffe eats more, **A** or **B**?

_____

Task 3

Each bucket holds 1 litre of water.

Giraffe **A** drank this many litres of water:

Giraffe **B** drank this many litres of water:

a How much water did each giraffe drink?

Giraffe **A** _____

Giraffe **B** _____

b Which giraffe drank less?

_____

WILD FACT

To take a drink, giraffes have to do the splits!

WILD FACT

Giraffes are the tallest animals in the world. They may have very long necks but, surprisingly, they have only 7 neck bones — the same number as you!

Now stride over to pages 28–29 and fill in your explorer's logbook!

Understanding time

Time is measured in **seconds**, **minutes** and **hours**. A second is the smallest unit of time.

Seconds add up to minutes and minutes add up to hours.

The **short hand** on a clock face tells us what hour it is.

The **long hand** tells us how many minutes to or past the hour it is.

Longer units of time include, **days**, **months** and **years**. **7 days** is equal to 1 **week**. 4 weeks is 1 **month** and there are **12** months in a **year**.

 When the **long hand** is pointing at 12 and the **short hand** points to another number, this is **o'clock**. The time on this clock is 5 o'clock.

 When the **long hand** is pointing at 6 and the **short hand** is halfway between two numbers, the time is **half past the hour**. The short hand on this clock is between 9 and 10, so it is showing a time of half past 9.

Task 1　Draw the hands on these clocks to show the following times that the baboons took a rest.

a 3 o'clock　　**b** 10 o'clock　　**c** 2 o'clock

WILD FACT

Baby baboons sometimes take a ride on their mother's back!

Task 2

Draw the hands on the clock faces to show the times that the baboons were grooming.

a Half past 7   **b** Half past 9   **c** Half past 4

Baboons spend hours grooming each other, which helps them to make and keep friends.

Task 3

a Baby baboons spend their first 2 months clinging to their mothers. How many weeks is this?

_____ weeks.

b Show how you worked this out:

_____

_____

Now walk over to pages 28–29 and fill in your explorer's logbook!

Two- and three-dimensional shapes

FACT FILE

Animal: African elephant
I live in: Grassland and savannah of Africa
I am: Up to 4 metres tall!
I eat: Grasses, roots and fruit

There are two main kinds of **shape**: **flat** or two-dimensional (**2D**) shapes and **solid** or three-dimensional (**3D**) shapes.

This is a **triangle**, it is a **2D** shape.

This is a **cube**, it is a **3D** shape.

WILD FACT

Elephants use their long noses, known as trunks, in lots of ways. They smell, eat and drink with them, and even use them as a snorkel to breathe through when they cross deep rivers!

Task 1

Look at these 2D shapes. Draw a line to match the shape to its name. One has been done for you.

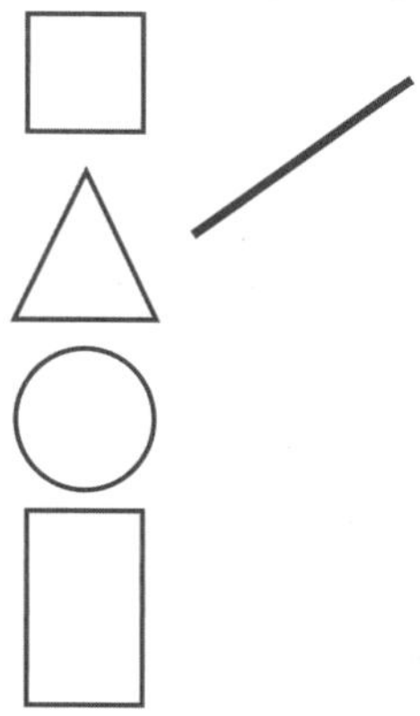

Triangle

Square

Rectangle

Circle

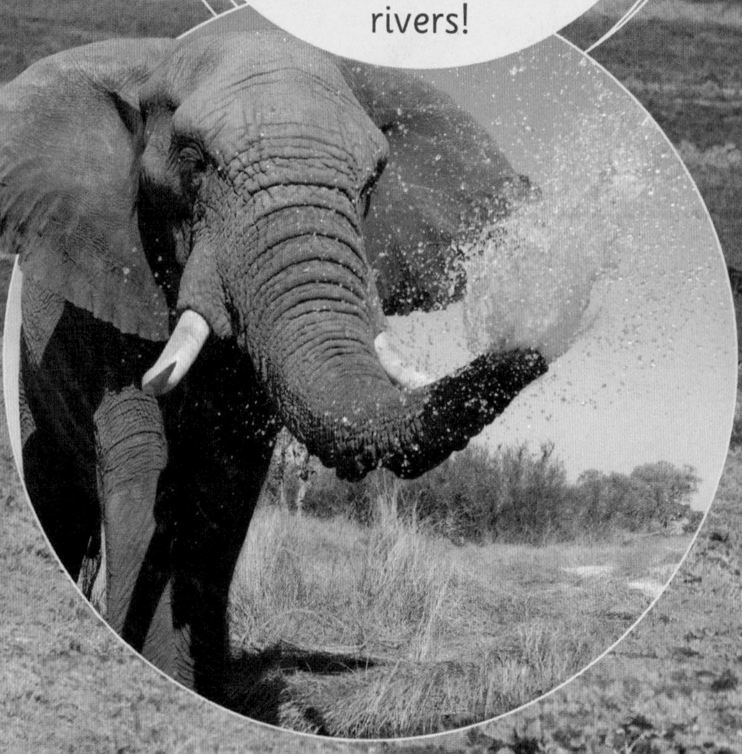

Task 2

Using the names in the box, write the name of the 3D shape next to its picture.

cylinder   cuboid   cone   pyramid

a _____

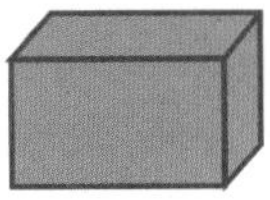

b _____

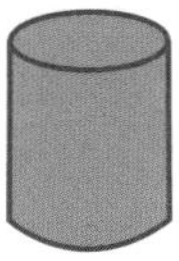

c _____

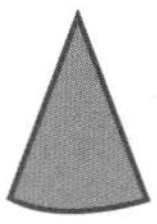

d _____

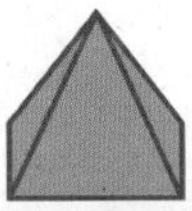

Task 3

Are these shapes 2D or 3D? Tick the correct box for each one.

	2D	3D
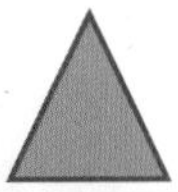		
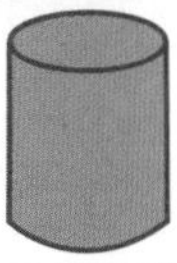		
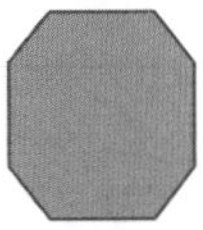		
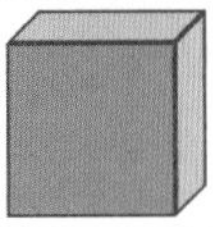		

Now stroll over to pages 28–29 and fill in your explorer's logbook!

Money

Being able to understand money is an important skill. Money can be either coins or notes. The different coins and notes each have their own value. Money is used to pay for things.

FACT FILE

Animal: Honey badger
I live in: Deserts, grasslands and woodlands of Africa and Asia
I weigh: Up to 14 kg
I eat: Honey, insects, fruit and small animals

WILD FACT

Don't frighten a honey badger! When scared, it can release an awful stink from under its tail to frighten away predators.

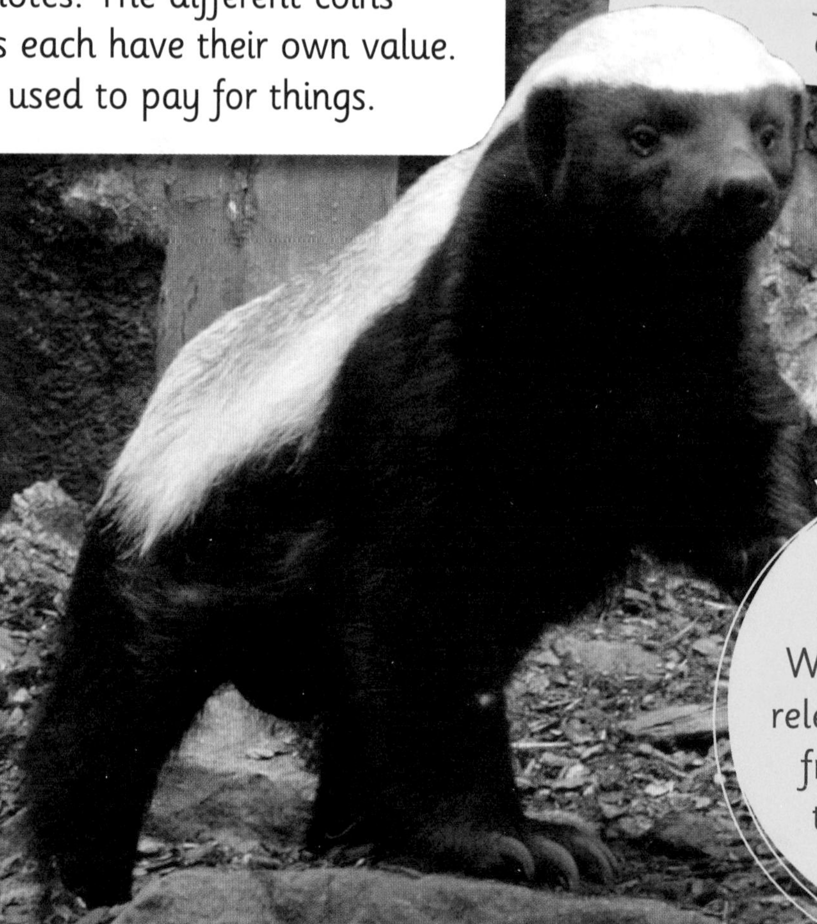

Task 1 Each honey pot costs 2p. How much would you have to pay for these honey pots altogether?

a

= ________p

b

= ________p

c

= ________p

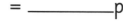

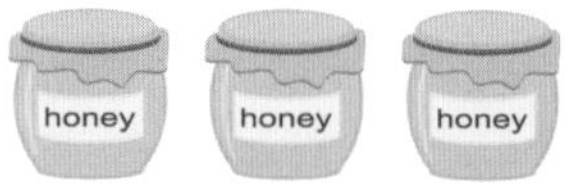

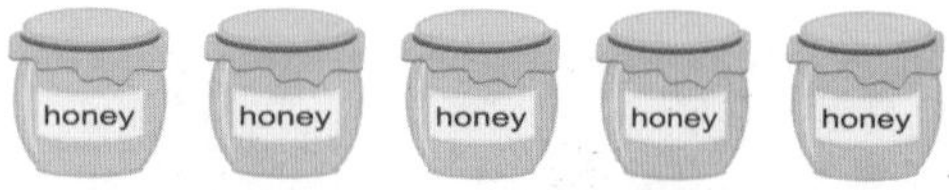

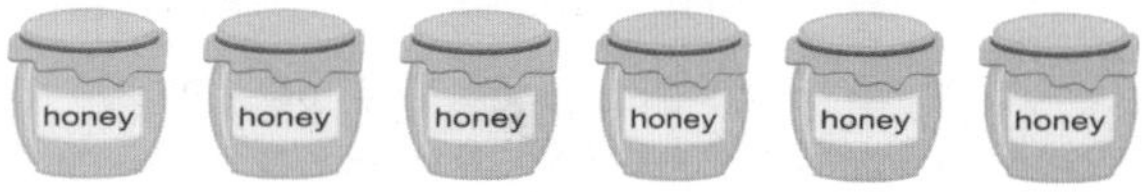

Task 2

A pot of honey costs 10p. Here are some of the coins that can be used to pay for the honey. The coins all have different values.

Write three different ways of making 10p from the coins above. You can use any combination of the coins. You can use more than one coin of the same value.

_____ = 10p

_____ = 10p

_____ = 10p

WILD FACT

Honey badgers may be small but they are fearsome fighters! They use their powerful jaws and strong claws to fight off predators and other honey badgers.

Task 3   Here are some coins.

£2   £1   20p   50p

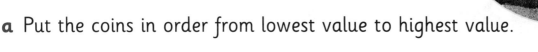

a Put the coins in order from lowest value to highest value.

Lowest _____ **Highest**

b How many 2p coins would have the same value as one 10p coin?

_____

c How many 10p coins would have the same value as one 50p coin?

_____

Now dig your way over to pages 28–29 and fill in your explorer's logbook!

Quick test

Now try these questions. Give yourself 1 mark for every correct answer.

1 **Put these numbers in order of value from lowest to highest.**
   12   7   14   3   5   _____ ☐

2 **Which of these numbers has the highest value?**
   Put a circle round it.
   12   17   11   19 ☐

3 **Put a circle round the number which has the lowest value.**
   13   15   18   10 ☐

4 **Write this as a multiplication.**
   $5 + 5 + 5 + 5$ _____ ☐

5 **Write this as a repeated addition.**
   2×4 _____ ☐

6 **Write the answer.**
   $10 \div 2 =$ _____ ☐

7 **Check this addition by using a subtraction.**
   $6 + 4 = 10$ _____ ☐

8 **Check this subtraction by using an addition.**
   $12 - 7 = 5$ _____ ☐

9 **How many hyenas equal half ($\frac{1}{2}$) of this clan?**

   _____ ☐

10 **What is a quarter ($\frac{1}{4}$) of 8?**   _____ ☐

11 **The baboons spent 1 hour each day grooming.**
   How many hours did they groom each
   other in 5 days?   _____ ☐

12 **Put these weights in order from lightest to heaviest.**

   12 kg   1 kg   10 kg   3 kg   _____ ☐

13 Here is a clock face showing the time now.

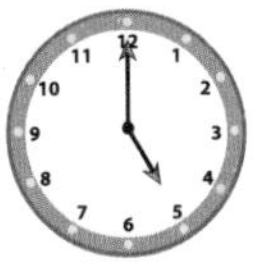

What time will it be in 1 hour? Draw the hands on the clock.

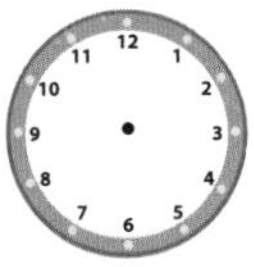

14 Which of these shapes is **NOT** a triangle?

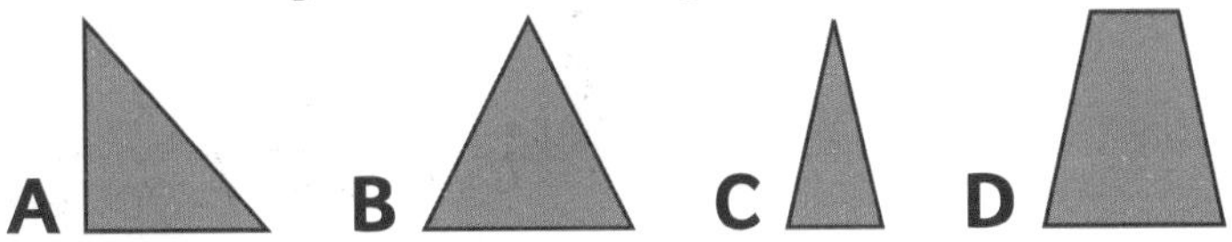

A   B   C   D   _____

15 What is the name of this 3D shape?

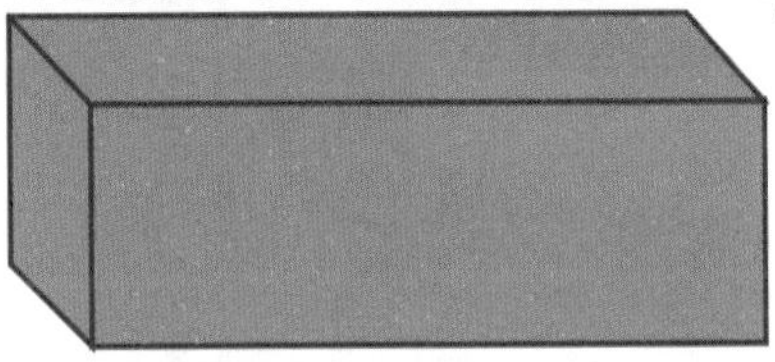

_____

16 Which shape is the odd one out? Tick the correct box.

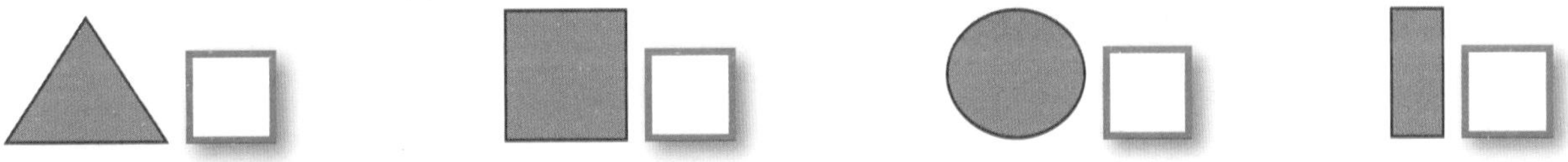

17 Why did you choose the shape that you ticked in question 16?

_____

18 Which of the coins shown below has the highest value?

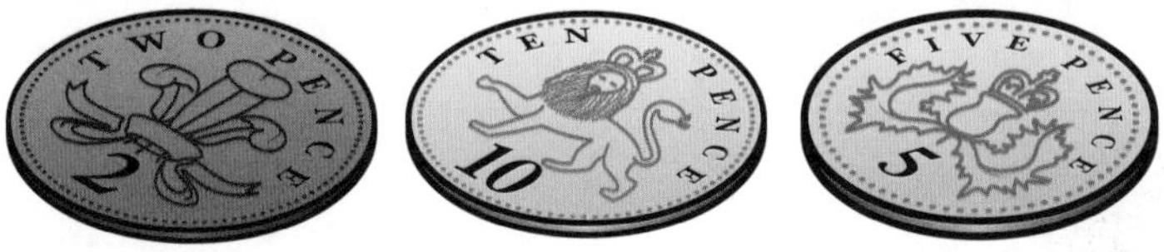

_____

19 Which of the coins shown above has the lowest value?

_____

20 What is the total of all of the coins shown above?

_____

Explorer's Logbook

Tick off the topics as you complete them and then colour in the star.

Place value ☐

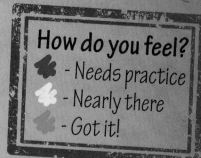

Ordering numbers ☐

More ordering numbers ☐

Writing numbers ☐

Multiplication ☐

Division ☐

Checking your maths ☐

Fractions ☐

Measuring ☐

Understanding time ☐

Two- and three-dimensional shapes ☐

Money ☐

Answers

Pages 2–3

Task 1

a 23   **b** 35   **c** 42

Task 2

a Any number that uses any 2 of the available digits, e.g. 12, 31, 43, 24

b 43

c 12

Task 3

a 6   **b** 20   **c** 7

d 70   **e** 40   **f** 90

Pages 4–5

Task 1

a 3, 5   **b** 5, 7   **c** 8, 10

Task 2

a 15   **b** 30   **c** 23   **d** 14

Task 3

1 less		1 more
55	56	57
33	34	35
20	21	22
1	2	3
12	13	14
72	73	74
54	55	56

Pages 6–7

Task 1

a 3, 12, 14, 26, 32

b 2, 7, 13, 29, 45

c 3, 16, 21, 23, 60

d 10, 13, 43, 51, 54

Task 2

a 10, 8, 6, 3, 2

b 34, 20, 18, 16, 4

c 51, 39, 27, 16, 5

Task 3

12, 14, 16, 18, 20 ✓

Task 4

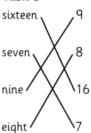

Pages 8–9

Task 1

a eight   **b** six   **c** twelve   **d** three

Task 2

a 5   **b** 20   **c** 11   **d** 1

Task 3

sixteen — 9
seven — 8
nine — 16
eight — 7

(lines cross: sixteen→16, seven→7, nine→9, eight→8)

Task 4

a seven   **c** twenty-one

b fourteen   **d** forty-three

Pages 10–11

Task 1

a $5 + 5 + 5$ or $3 + 3 + 3 + 3 + 3$

b $10 + 10 + 10 + 10 + 10$ or $5 + 5 + 5 + 5 + 5 + 5 + 5 + 5 + 5 + 5$

c $2 + 2 + 2 + 2 + 2 + 2$ or $6 + 6$

Task 2

a 10×5 or 5×10

b 2×7 or 7×2

c 5×7 or 7×5

Task 3

a 10   **b** 60   **c** 16

Task 4

a $3 \times 5 = 15$ **c** $4 \times 4 = 16$

b $6 \times 2 = 12$ **d** $6 \times 3 = 18$

Pages 12–13

Task 1

a $2 \div 2 = 1$ **c** $12 \div 2 = 6$

b $4 \div 2 = 2$ **d** $14 \div 2 = 7$

Task 2

$10 \div 2 = 5$

Task 3

a 2   **b** 3   **c** 6

Pages 14–15

Task 1

a $3 - 1 = 2$

b $7 - 1 = 6$

c $10 - 6 = 4$

Task 2

a $6 \div 2 = 3$ **b** $8 \div 2 = 4$ **c** $12 \div 2 = 6$

Task 3

a $12 - 10 = 2$ **b** $5 \times 2 = 10$ **c** $10 + 10 = 20$

Pages 16–17

Task 1

a   **b**

Task 2

a 3   b 4   c 5

Task 3

a 1   b 2   c 3

Pages 18–19

Task 1

Giraffe A is taller

Task 2

a Giraffe A eats 3 kg, giraffe B eats 4 kg

b Giraffe B

Task 3

a Giraffe A drank 9 litres, giraffe B drank 7 litres

b Giraffe B

Pages 20–21

Task 1

 a   b   c

Task 2

 a   b   c

Task 3

a 8 weeks

b 1 month = 4 weeks, so 2 months = 2 × 4 = 8 weeks

Pages 22–23

Task 1

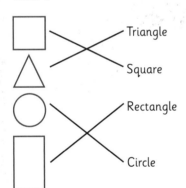

Task 2

a cuboid   b cylinder

c cone   d pyramid

Task 3

	2D	3D
△	✓	
cylinder		✓
octagon	✓	
cube		✓

Pages 24–25

Task 1

a 6p   b 10p   c 12p

Task 2

Any combination of available coins, e.g. 10 × 1p, 2 × 5p, 5p + 2p + 2p + 1p

Task 3

a 20p, 50p, £1, £2

b 5

c 5

Pages 26–27

1 3, 5, 7, 12, 14

2 19

3 10

4 5 × 4

5 2 + 2 + 2 + 2

6 5

7 10 − 4 = 6

8 5 + 7 = 12

9 3 hyenas

10 2

11 5 hours

12 1 kg, 3 kg, 10 kg, 12 kg

13

14 D

15 cuboid

16   ✓

17 It has no straight sides/edges

18 10p

19 2p

20 17p

Well done, explorer!

You have finished your maths adventure!

Explorer's pass

Name: _____

Age: _____

Date: _____

Draw a picture of yourself in the box!